G000230470

THE
Old Photographs
SERIES

PADSTOW

Pockett's Bristol Channel Steam Packet Co., Ltd

INCREASED SAILINGS.

VELINDRA, RIO FORMOSO & COLLIER

MAY 1893.

Will Sail as follows, if not prevented by any unforeseen occurrence, with liberty to Tow Vessels—Between

Bristol, Swansea, Ilfracombe & Padstow,

For the Month of MAY, 1893.

Swansea and Bristol.

FROM SWANSEA.				FROM BRISTOL.			
MONDAY,	May 1...	7 30	after	TUESDAY, May 2...	7 0	after
TUESDAY,	2...	8 0	after	THURSDAY,	4...	8 0	after
THURSDAY,	4...	9 0	morn	SATURDAY,	6...	9 0	after
SATURDAY,	6...	10 0	morn	TUESDAY,	9...12 0	night
TUESDAY,	9...12 30	noon	THURSDAY,	11...	2 0	after
WEDNESDAY,	10...12 0	night	FRIDAY,	12...	3 0	after
FRIDAY,	12... 4 0	after	SATURDAY,	13...	3 30	after
MONDAY,	15... 6 30	after	TUESDAY,	16...	6 0	after
TUESDAY,	16... 7 30	after	THURSDAY,	18...	7 30	after
THURSDAY,	18... 8 30	morn	SATURDAY,	20...	9 0	after
SATURDAY,	20...10 30	morn	WEDNESDAY,	24...	2 0	after
TUESDAY,	23... 1 0	after	THURSDAY,	25...	3 0	after
THURSDAY,	25... 3 30	after	SATURDAY,	27...	4 0	after
MONDAY,	29... 6 30	after	TUESDAY,	30...	6 0	after

All Goods conveyed from Bristol to Swansea insured at Lloyd's without expense to senders or consignees. Order "PER POCKETT."

Goods for Swansea received daily at 11, Narrow Quay, Bristol.

Goods for Bristol received daily at South Dock Entrance, Swansea

Swansea and Ilfracombe.

FROM SWANSEA.				FROM ILFRACOMBE.			
MONDAY,	May 15...	7 0	morn	MONDAY, May 15...	5 30	after
TUESDAY,	16...	7 0	morn	TUESDAY,	16...	6 0	after
WEDNESDAY,	17...	7 0	morn	WEDNESDAY,	17...	6 0	after
THURSD'Y,	18...	8 0	morn	THURSD'Y,	18...	6 0	after
FRIDAY,	19...	7 0	morn	FRIDAY,	19...	6 0	after
SATURDAY,	20...	7 0	morn	SATURDAY,	20...	6 0	after
MONDAY,	22...	8 0	morn	MONDAY,	22...	6 0	afte,
TUESDAY,	23...	9 15	morn	TUESDAY,	23...	7 0	after
WEDNESDAY,	24...10 15	morn	WEDNESDAY,	24...	1 15	after
THURSDAY,	26...	2 30	after	THURSDAY,	25...	8 30	after
SATURDAY,	27...	1 0	after	SATURDAY,	27...	4 0	after
MONDAY,	29...	7 0	morn	MONDAY,	29...	5 30	after
TUESDAY,	30...	7 0	morn	TUESDAY,	30...	6 0	afte,
WEDNESDAY,	31...	7 0	morn	WEDNESDAY,	31...	6 0	after

FARES :—SINGLE, Best Cabin, 4/6 ; Fore Cabin, 3/- ;
RETURN, (available for one month,) Best Cabin, 7/- ;
Fore Cabin, 5/-.

Bristol and Ilfracombe.
GOODS ONLY.

FROM BRISTOL.				FROM ILFRACOMBE.			
TUESDAY,	May 2...	7 0	after	WE'NSDAY, May 3...	4 0	morn
TUESDAY,	9...12 0	night	WEDNESDAY,	10...	7 0	morn
TUESDAY,	16... 6 0	after	WEDNESDAY,	17...	4 0	morn
THURSDAY,	25... 3 0	after	FRIDAY,	26...	7 0	morn
TUESDAY,	30... 6 0	after	WEDNESDAY,	31...	4 0	morn

Bristol, Padstow and Wadebridge.

CALLING AT SWANSEA.

FROM BRISTOL				FROM PADSTOW.			
FRIDAY, April 28...	4 0	after	MONDAY, May 1...	5 0	after
FRIDAY, May 12...	3 0	after	MONDAY,	15...	4 30	after
THURSDAY,	25... 3 0	after	MONDAY,	29...	4 30	after

NOTICE.—All Goods for Padstow and Wadebridge must be alongside before 6 p.m. on the day before Sailing.

Swansea, Padstow and Wadebridge.

FROM SWANSEA.				FROM PADSTOW.			
SAT'RD'Y, April 29...	3 30	after	MONDAY, May 1...	5 0	after
SATURD'Y, May 13...	2 0	after	MONDAY,	15...	4 30	after
FRIDAY,	26... 1 15	after	MONDAY,	29...	4 30	after

London and South Western trains leave Ilfracombe for Barnstaple, Bideford, &c., at 7.35 a.m., 9.30 a.m., 10.25 a.m., 12.25 a.m., 2.5 p.m., 4.40 p.m., 7.25 p.m.

FOR FURTHER PARTICULARS APPLY TO

SWANSEA—H. Knill, Entrance South Dock.
BRISTOL—T. Probert, 11 Narrow Quay, General Manager.
ILFRACOMBE—J. W. Smyth, Steam Packet Office, Pier or Quay.
PADSTOW & WADEBRIDGE—Thomas Cavell, Wadebridge.
BIDEFORD—London and South Western Station.
BARNSTAPLE—Chaplin & Co., Joy Street.

PLYMOUTH—J. Wainwright & Son, Westwell Street.
LONDON—London and South Western Railway Company, Waterloo Station.
And all Stations and Offices of the London and South Western Railway Company.
London and North Western Railway Company, Euston Station.
And all Stations and Offices of the London and North Western Railway Company.

The Owners give notice that they will not receive any Passengers, Persons, Animals or Goods, for conveyance or otherwise, under any circumstances whatsoever except under the express terms and conditions that such Owners shall not in any way be responsible for any loss, injury, damage, whatsoever, and from whatever cause arising, of or to, or in relation to such Passengers, Persons, Animals, or Goods, respectively, while the same shall be in the possession, custody, care or charge of the Owners or their Agents or Servants, or on any Quay, Wharf or Place on which they may be placed, landed, or kept ; nor for the acts, neglects, or defaults of any Railway Canal or other company, Carrier, or Party, to whom they may be passed on in the ordinary course of reception, carriage, detention, transit or delivery—The Proprietors will not hold themselves liable for the Dangers and Accidents of the Sea of any kind or description, whatsoever or howsoever, The Owners reserve to themselves the power to omit or alter any of their advertised sailings, with or without previous notice, and will not be liable for any loss, damage or expenses which may accrue to any

A poster advertising the steam packet ships which ran from Bristol to Padstow. The *Collier*, one of the vessels mentioned, is illustrated on page 55.

THE
Old Photographs
SERIES

PADSTOW

Compiled by
Malcolm McCarthy

CHALFORD

BATH · AUGUSTA · RENNES

First published 1994
Copyright © Malcolm McCarthy, 1994

The Chalford Publishing Company Limited
St Mary's Mill, Chalford, Stroud
Gloucestershire GL6 8NX

ISBN 0 7524 0033 9

Typesetting and origination
by Alan Sutton Limited
Printed in Great Britain

Liberated Edwardian women socialize in the grounds of Prideaux Place.

Contents

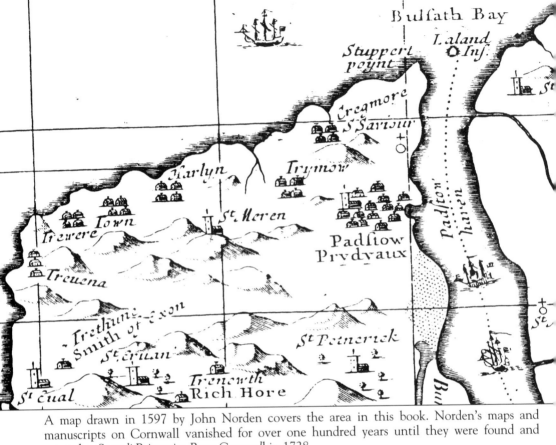

A map drawn in 1597 by John Norden covers the area in this book. Norden's maps and manuscripts on Cornwall vanished for over one hundred years until they were found and printed as *Speculi Britanniae Pars: Cornwall* in 1728.

DEDICATION

To all those who have gone before us, without whom this book would not have been possible.

Introduction

In 1977 I started to collect old photographs, postcards and snaps of Padstow and district. This fuelled my enthusiasm and my collection has grown steadily with the generous help of many individuals. Now I have not only photographs, but Cornish and local books, original documents dating back to 1656, newspaper cuttings, posters, and other ephemera, all helping to build a picture of Padstow in days gone by.

Since the appearance of my last book, many people have expressed great interest and encouraged me to produce another; this I have done out of a sense of duty to all those who have helped me over the years. I hope that my putting names to faces will mean this book becomes a useful document, as with every passing year there are fewer people able to help me identify their classmates – a sobering thought.

I take this opportunity to thank all those who have helped and are still helping me to collect and collate this useful and historic material. I have compiled this book in the hope that it will in turn prove helpful to future generations.

Some individuals think I am making my fortune by producing these books, so let me assure everyone that every penny which comes to me from their sale is spent on enhancing the collection.

I hope that the publication brings pleasure to one and all, from Padstow to Peru, from St Merryn to Sydney.

Malcolm McCarthy
Padstow
June 1994

Inspector Crocker on the left and PC Rawlings stand with an unidentified female in the Market, c. 1925. The police station at this time was in Church Lane.

One
Wreck and Rescue

Lifeboat Day about 1902. Alongside the slip is the surf lifeboat *Edmund Harvey* and laying off is the *Arab*. The slip being used is the one beside the present day Sailing Club; it now has walls on both sides. Apart from the landscape, everything else in the photograph has changed.

Launching the pre-1901 *Arab* from the boathouse at Cove. Everybody lent a hand to launch the boat, especially in emergencies, as is illustrated by this extract from a newspaper article when the Milford trawler *Birdie* went aground on the Doom Bar in a gale: "Hawkers Cove, where the Padstow lifeboat is stationed, is two miles from the town, and when the signal gun was heard the only people at the Cove were the wives and daughters of the Trinity Pilots. While the crew were flying from Padstow to the Cove, these eight women and girls hauled the *Arab* out of the lifeboat house, ran her down the slipway, and running kneehigh into the rough sea, got her successfully launched by the time the men arrived." The *Birdie* and all her crew were consequently saved.

A series of three photographs illustrating the launching of the *Arab*. The lifeboat is pulled stern first on its trolley from the lifeboat house at Cove to the beach at Harlyn by a team of horses.

Horses pull the *Arab* on its trolley in an arc through the surf to position it for launching.

Arab is slipped off its trolley bow first; the trolley pulled from under the boat by horses leaves the vessel free to row seaward.

The second *Arab*; this 10-oared 35 ft long self-righting lifeboat served from 1901 to 1931, being launched 26 times and saving 68 lives. Coxswain William Baker is standing in the stern of the boat.

The wreck of the *Arab* on the rocks at Greenaway. The *Arab* had gone to the aid of the Lowestoft trawling ketch *Peace and Plenty*, which had dragged her anchor from under Stepper towards Greenaway Rocks in a strong WNW gale. Four of the crew were saved by rocket apparatus from Trebetherick; one man swam ashore, three others were drowned. The *Arab* had gone to her assistance but, unable to find her, was overcome by the huge seas running. Having lost most of her oars, the anchor was put out and she was eventually carried onto the Greenaway Rocks with all her crew scrambling to safety. The RNLB *James Stevens* coming to the *Arab's* aid was also overcome by the sea and wrecked with the tragic loss of eight of her eleven man crew.

Lifeboat day, August 1907 as described by part of a newspaper article. "A lifeboat demonstration on Saturday, despite the unsuitable day, attracted a record number of sightseers. Lifeboat rockets bursting over the town marked the commencement of the proceedings. The steam lifeboat *Helen Peele*, the surf lifeboat *Edmund Harvey* and the *Arab*, the self-righting lifeboat, were fully manned and exercised at the quay, and were open to public inspection. On the South quay a life saving demonstration was carried out by means of an improvised apparatus. The hulk *Swift* was moored off as a wreck with sailors on board. No rockets being available for carrying a line to the wreck, a 'sound' rocket was fired, and it was left to the imagination that communication had been effected. When the first man was landed the strain of the hawser caused the wreck to drag her anchor, the sailor in the breeches buoy falling into the sea, to the amusement of the onlookers." The three boats then went to Wadebridge for a demonstration; unfortunately, the *Helen Peele* hit the quay breaking two blades off her propeller.

RNLI steam tug lifeboat *Helen Peele*. In this photograph the lifeboat is aground, a matter of concern for some as illustrated by this letter from a local newspaper of the time: "Sir, in all the records of disaster and shipwreck on the North Coast of Cornwall, October claims a larger share of tragedies then any other month. The weather at the present time is stormy and unsettled in the extreme, yet this is the time chosen to dock the fine steamer lifeboat *Helen Peele* for survey and painting. Last winter a correspondent called attention in your columns to the fact that this lifeboat was four hours in getting to sea after a signal of distress through the same cause. Will the authorities never learn anything from experience?" Signed, Disgusted.

In the foreground is the RNLB *Princess Mary*, a gift to the RNLI by the P&O group. To the east of the lifeboat is the French three-masted topsail schooner *Marie Regina*, the last sailing vessel to be wrecked on the Bar, where she met her fate on 2nd March 1932. Her wreck was bought by Arthur Reveley for £5 on behalf of himself, Bill Orchard, Norman England, Oscar Martyn and Jim and Harry Brenton. She was blown in under Tregirls cliffs where she was stripped of fixtures and fittings, and her useful timbers salvaged. The barge *Beaumaris* was used to transport the spoils to Brabyn's Yard, where it was brought ashore, taken to Langford's Quay, and sold by auction a few weeks later.

The RNLB *Princess Mary* was on service at Padstow from 1929–1952, being launched 63 times and saving 68 lives. The crew of the boat are: in the stern, Philip May, John Tallack Murt (coxswain), Nick Reynolds, and Ernie Murt at the bow. The *Princess Mary* was a twin screw Barnett lifeboat, 61 ft long with a 15 ft beam, her top speed being 9½ knots. The *Princess Mary* was sold by the RNLI in 1954 and became the yacht *Aries R*. She was the first small, powered craft to make a double crossing of the Atlantic without the use of sails.

14

The RNLB *John and Sarah Eliza Stych* on sea trials when new, prior to coming to Padstow. She was a self-righting lifeboat, 35½ ft long with a top speed of 7⅓ knots. During her eight years at Padstow she was launched only seven times, saving eight lives.

The RNLB *John and Sarah Eliza Stych* ablaze on the rocks at Godrevy. This lifeboat was on loan from Padstow to St Ives. The *Stych* had been launched at 3a.m. on the 22nd January 1939 to aid a steamer in trouble two miles north of Cape Cornwall in a WNW storm force 10. During her efforts to reach the steamer she capsized and six of her seven crew drowned. The steamer, whose name was never known, came within a few hundred yards of the cliffs at St Just, when she managed to make to seaward, and safety.

The RNLB *Bassett Green* was on service at Padstow from 1951–1962, being launched 79 times and saving 115 lives. The crew of the boat are: Harry Brenton in the stern, Horace Murt at the wheel, Bill Bray with back to camera and Dick and Walter Bate to left of the Mast.

The RNLB *Joseph Hiram Chadwick* was on service at Padstow from 1952–1967, being launched 91 times and saving 51 lives. The crew of the vessel are, from left to right: Philip May, John Tallack Murt (at the wheel), Nick Reynolds, and Ernie Murt. The vessel was 52 ft long, of Barnett type, with twin 60hp diesel engines capable of 8 knots.

The RNLB *James and Catherine MacFarlane*. The crew: Ian Kendall, Sid Porter, Chris Hughes, Alf Prosser, Ricky Tummon, Trevor England, Peter Poole, Steven Thomas, Arthur May. The *James and Catherine* was an Oakley type lifeboat with two 110 hp diesel engines, 48 ft 6 in long with a 14 ft beam. She remained in service until being replaced by the present boat, the RNLB *James Burrough*, on 15th April 1985.

The Board of Trade rocket apparatus wagon at Mother Ivey's Bay. A controversial incident is described in a newspaper of 1903 which states: "Last night during a strong gale of wind, with rain, the whole town was alarmed by rockets being fired for the crews of the lifeboat. Being a member of the Rocket Brigade, and having retired for the night, I hurriedly dressed, and running and walking, got to the rocket house, a distance of two miles over one of the most dangerous roads to travel by night that exists in the County, there to learn that it was only 'a surprise practice' for the lifeboat; also the information from the Commanding Officer of the Coastguard, that the brigade was not called and he supposed I came down for the pleasure. I replied that it was impossible for anyone to form any idea as to the nature of the explosive used when startled out of their sleep at night. Nearly all the members of the Rocket Brigade were there....' The letter is signed W. Philp, 17th December, Padstow.

The 264 ton three masted schooner *Petrel* of Leith carrying oil and marble from Leghorn to Belfast wrecked in Wine Cove near Treyarnon Bay on Thursday 9th December 1886. The mate stated: "We left Leghorn on the 24th of October, and all went well with us until Wednesday morning when we encountered a WNW gale, during which we lost all our sails, boats, and bulwarks. On Thursday morning we tried to weather Trevose Head, but failed, and were driven before the gale right onto the rock-bound shore. At the entrance to Wine Cove we struck on some rocks and the crew took to the rigging. The mainmast was carried away and Captain Willas who was clinging to it was drowned. A tremendous sea then struck her and carried her stern first right into the cove." Two of the crew scaled the cliffs and the other four were rescued by the local farmers.

The wreck of the Falmouth schooner *Jessie McClew* bound from Porthcawl to Penzance with coal. She drove ashore at Booby's Bay in October 1895. The crew under the command of Captain J.H. Carbines of St Ives, pulled ashore, surfing in on the back of a breaker.

Ashore in Mother Ivey's Bay on 21st April 1906, the ketch *Belt* of Beaumaris 150 tons burthen from St Agnes to Chester River with 120 tons of nitro-cake. The vessel was under the command of the owner's father, Captain Foulkes. On leaving St Agnes after undergoing extensive repairs she struck the pier heavily several times. Soon it became apparent that the vessel was leaking badly and that water was rapidly gaining on the pumps. A distress signal was hoisted, and eventually, to prevent the vessel foundering in deep water, she was run ashore and beached, there being several feet of water in her hold. During the night, ground sea battered the uninsured *Belt*, leaving her to end her days on the beach.

The French brigantine *Angele*, wrecked on the Doom Bar on the morning of 12th November 1911. On this fateful morning the schooner *Island Maid* was also lost on the Bar. The lifeboat was unable to rescue the crew of the *Angele* when she grounded due to the shallow water. With enormous seas breaking, and the crew being exhausted from saving the latter, coxswain William Baker, with a volunteer crew put off in the *Arab* and saved the Captain of the vessel. Coxswain Baker was awarded the RNLI Silver Medal for his part in this rescue.

19

Crowds gather to see the Swansea brigantine *Industry* wrecked on 12th September 1912 in Harlyn Bay. She was carrying coal bound from Briton Ferry to Treport. Some of her ribs can still be seen at times near Harlyn Bridge.

Another photograph of the *Industry*. Men are on her deck, possibly seeing what could be saved. Both the coastguard and customs were vigilant regarding items being brought illegally ashore; anyone caught was liable to arrest.

The 1,993 ton steel ship *Carl* of Hamburg aground in Booby's Bay 7th October 1917. She was built in 1893 and ended her days on the sands, despite the efforts of a pair of Admiralty tugs from Falmouth. The *Carl* regularly uncovers and great lengths of her steel ribs are exposed.

The Yarmouth steam trawler *Smiling Thro'* ashore at Rocky Beach, Trevone in April 1924.

Launched in 1916 at Newcastle and then called the *Scotol*, this naval oiler was sold in 1948 to Hemsley Bell Ltd. of Southampton, who changed her name to *Hemsley I*. She worked right up to 1969, when on her way to a breaker's yard she went ashore at Fox Cove, Treyarnon in a southerly gale.

The Brixham beam trawler BM.235 *Sea Image* on the Town Bar, 8th March 1992. The skipper Mark "Pinky" George can be seen surveying his plight. The vessel leaving on an ebb tide misjudged the channel and spent the day on the sand. She came off without any damage, though there was slight panic as the crew, who had waded ashore, lost track of time, and returned to find their vessel surrounded by water and no immediate means of boarding her.

Two
Just People

Padstow Brownies, c. 1937. Back row: Heather Porter, Margaret Sleeman, Bubbles Phillips, Mildred Reynolds. Third row: Eileen Bate, Hilda Ainscough, Sylvia George, -?-, Nora Prout, Nancy Crowther. Centre row: Adela Lobb, -?-, -?-. The rest: Trixie Edyvane, Peggy Hornabrook, Evelyn Kinsmen, Peggy Walker, Betty Phillips, Jean Fuller and Joyce Lobb.

The workers at Stepper Point Quarry, c. 1910. Back row: Robert England, Stan Magor, Will Old, Fred Pinch, Sam Bragg, Bill Porter, Will Thomas. Middle row: Oscar Kane, Harry Cox. Front row: Percy Bishop, Will Watson, Eddie Bruford and Albert Courtney.

Padstow Band, c. 1907. Back row: H. Apps, F. Sluman, Alf Buckingham, Joe Buckingham, Edgar Tonkin, Sid Tonkin, Alf Langford, Stanley Veale, Sidney Sleeman. Sitting: John Buckingham, Willie Veale, George Buckingham, T. Chellew, Tom Langford, Harvey Lobb, Willie Lobb. Reclining: Joe Williams and Albert Courteney. The Padstow Band, a source of enjoyment to many, was not appreciated by everyone, as can be seen from the following letter printed in the *Western Morning News*, 28th June 1872: "'Somnolency' writes from Padstow to suggest to the members of the Padstow Volunteer Band that whilst the practise of blowing their instruments in the streets at midnight is doubtless very amusing to themselves, it may not be equally gratifying to all their neighbours."

Padstow 2nd Girl Guides at St Georges, c. 1926. Back row; -?-, -?-, Lorna Holloway, Jessie Porter, May Brenton, Mary Magor, Hilda Rolling, Rose Ellery. Fourth row: Adela Lobb, Phyllis Bate, Marion Wright. Third row: -?-, Pat Derrick, Violet Soper, Maisey Mortley, Cathy Martyn. Second row: Bessie Rawe, Amy Trenouth, Betty Mabley, Molly Reynolds, believed a Cribbens, Hilda Berry, Violet Grubb, Myrtle Dawe, Marjorie Thomas. Front row: Betty Clark, Eleanor Duffy, May Coombes, Joan Oldham, Maisie Pope, Audrey Chidgey, Lady Vyvyan and Elfreda Hornabrook.

The Orpheus Male Voice Quartet proudly show some of their trophies. Harold Ball, Frank Bray, Fred Magor and Loveridge Lobb.

The Cheerio's, c. 1917. Nellie Bate, Ella Chapman, Louie Cowl (later Ravenhill), Evelyn Bate, Emily Bate (later Rowe), Olive Bate (later Brabyn), Doris Sluman (later Pope), Dora Bate (later Dives), and Hettie ? (surname unknown). Nellie and Evelyn were sisters and cousins to the three sisters Emily, Olive and Dora.

The Fairies from the D'arcy De Ferris production of *Robin Hood* of 1923. Back row: Maisie Pope, Winnie Brinham, Marion Rattenbury, Marjorie Hutchings, Nina Nicholson. Second row: Phyllis Bate, Ivy Hellier, Mary McOwen, Hilda Berry, Molly Reynolds, Doris Moore, May Coombes, Betty Chidgey. Front row: Phyllis Prior, Betty Mabley, Joan Oldham, Bubbles Harvey, Molly Honey and Agnes Rawe.

Padstow Boy's School, c. 1919. Back row: Ivan Blowers, Laurie Giddy, Frank Magor, Ronald Honey, George Bate, George Prior, Leonard Grubb. Third row; Jim Gard, Arthur Gard, George Pinch, George Brenton, Billy Porter, Reg Bate, Arthur Davies, Charlie Edwards, Les Davies, Bill Catt, Stanley Worsdell. Third row: Willie Thomas, Leonard Williams, Arnold Mabley, David Champion, Ron Worsdell, Jerry Dale, -?-, Arnold Fuller, Morris Cullum, Gordon Fuller. Front row: Jack O'Keefe, Albert Kitto, George Kitto, David Champion, Sam Lobb, Bill Thomas and Jack Reynolds.

Padstow Boys School, c. 1930. Back row: Jim Smith, Brenton Bate, Joe May, Roy Crews, Harry Tucker, Olaf Kane, Gordon Lenny, Percy Prior. Middle row: Edgar Fuller, Reg Murt, Len Cowling, -?-, Jim Edyvane, Doug Martyn, Henry Old, Jim Prior. Front row: Stanley Old, Jack Gard, Jack Bennett, Jack "Titch" England, Jim Taylor, Jack Phillips, George Giddy, Gordon Chidgey and Bob Davey.

Padstow Girls School, c. 1923. Back row: -?-, Phyllis Stone, Hilda Rosevear, Nora Alexander, Isabel Brown, Lena Kinsmen, Florence McOwen, Winnie Hill. Second row: May Coombes, Rose Ellery, Renee Fuller, Laura Bate, Muriel Davies, -?-, Phyllis Watson, Mary Giddy, Joan Oldham. Bottom row: Vera Brown, believed Phyllis Manley, Lorna Mabley, -?-, Mary Thomas, Edna Fuller, Bertha Brown, -?-, Cathy Martyn, Mary O'Keefe, -?-.

Padstow Girls School, c. 1925. Back row: Miss Jinny Angove (teacher), Violet Soper, Mary Rolling, Phyllis Bate, -?-, believed Phyllis Horn, Doris Mortley, Renée Rosevear, Molly Honey, May Coombes, Gwen Bennett. Second row: Eileen Rogers, believed Phyllis Manley, Bubbles Harvey, -?-, Betty Mabley, Phyllis Prior, Rose Ellery, Vida Brown, Muriel Davies, Louvaine Kinsmen, Bessie Bennett. Front row: Cathy Martyn, Marjorie Fuller, Margaret Giddy, Mary O'Keefe, Phyllis Dawe, -?-, Nora Alexander, Betsy Crapp and Vera Tresidder.

Padstow School Infants. Back row: Eleanor Grubb, -?-, Marjorie Magor, Edwina Moore, -?-, Kathleen O'Hagan. Middle row: Norman Williams, John Stuart, Clifford Hill, Tommy Criggan, Ray Brewer, Bert Dawe, Frank Masters, Arthur Gard. Front row: Clara Kitto, Bernice Brunyee, Betty Grubb, Mildred Ayres, Margaret Thomas, Margaret Sorensen, Gerald Dawe, -?-, Bob Dale.

St Merryn Council School, c. 1917. Back row, left to right: Miss Josephine Ford, a teacher, Alfred Bennett, Ernie Hawken, George Rabey, -?-, -?-, Percy Bray, Clarence Strongman, -?-, Thomas Albert Chapman, Mr Waddleton, the Headmaster. Second row: Mildred Sandry, -?-, Madeline Old, Arthur Old, Doris Brewer, Iris Strongman, -?-, Reg Geach. Front row: Roy Prynn, Emma Bennett, -?-, Gladys Geach, Hilda Brewer, Kathleen Sandry, Trixie Hawken, Phyllis Rosevear and Edwin Strongman.

St Merryn School, c. 1924. Back row: John Blake, Nick Curgenven, Jack Ingrey, Dennis Bennett, John Pitman, Charlie Pitman, Melrose Hawken, Mr Waddleton, the Headmaster. Middle row: Ernest Bennett, Jocelyn Duffy, Arthur "Fatty" Foster, Bert Walters. Front row: Ross Newcombe, Edith Bennett, Effie Hicks, Elsie Pinch, Evered Bennett, Josie Walters, Betty Geach and Leslie Bennett.

St Merryn School, 1938. Back row: Roger Backway, Howard Leverton, Eileen Roscorla, Florence Barrett, Avis Ellery, Ruth Damerel, Henry Morgan, Ivor Rawe. Third row: Billy Hawke, Dennis Kessell, Donald Trenerry, Reggie Bennett, Mabel Hawkins, Dinah Backway, Maureen Bryant, Phyllis Andrew, Joy Brewer, Sylvia Williams, Maureen Champion, Diana Funnell, Irving Ball, Roger Darke, Reggie Lethbridge, George Trenouth. Second row: Zoe Champion, Renée Trenouth, Estell Hawkins, Hilda Bennett, Margaret Yelland, -?-, Mr Nancarrow, the Headmaster, Miss Amy Rawe, Jean Ford, Eileen Hawke, June Bennett, Peggy Ford, -?-, -?-. Front row: Donald Cowling, Alec McCallan, Graham Ball, Llewelyn Morgan, David Saundry, Rex Trenouth, -?-, Eric Martyn.

Padstow Football Team, c. 1948. Back row: A. Hosgood, Jack Bennett, Gerald Bennett, Neil Burke, Tom Masters, Stanley Thomas, Stanley Conium, Arthur Brown, Harry Cox. Front row: David Allen, Johnny Allen, Roy Bate, Jimmy Tregembo, Tony Allen and Geoffrey Cox.

Two photographs of girls dressed up as a gypsy troupe, c. 1920. The pictures were taken in Stile Field and in the one on the left are: Nora Biddick, Kitty Magor, Dora Watts, Doris Hutchings, Marjorie Hawken, Nora Cowling, Doris Cribbens, Monica Old, Enid Hutchings, Mildred Prior. The back five in the picture on the right are: Winnie Couch, Kitty Magor, Doris Hutchings, Rita Stone, Ena Buckingham. The other three are: May Biddick, Nora Biddick and Lena Ricketts.

Padstow Church Choir. George Bate, Jack Stewart, Mr O'Keefe, Bill Tippett, Dennis Chapman, Gordon Dawe, Rev. Rust, Edward Davey and Mr Farwell.

SWEB staff outside their office on the North Quay in the early 1950's. Back row: Gordon Dawe, Reg Walters, Trevor Scantlebury, Neil Burke, Bernard Brebner, -?-, B. Newell, Jimmy Watson, Michael Hornabrook, Tom Carrick. Second row: Roy Bate, William John England, Geoff Hicks, Frank Mabley, Douglas Baseley, Kitchener Hoare, Harry Grubb, Leonard Prior. Sitting: Paddy Trevethan, Dora Hoblyn, Wally Gabbitas, John Pearson, Arnold Mabley and Albert Ellacott.

Three
The Railway

Awaiting the first train, 23rd March 1899. The men are supporting an illuminated scroll which is now in the Padstow Museum. They are: W. Derrick, Captain W.T. Hutchings, Captain Aaron Sloggett, Frank Sluman, Joseph Hicks, John Hicks, Johnson Tom, W. Betties, Thomas Tummon, Sandford Allport, John Sleeman, -?-, Mr Williams, Captain W. Pope, -?-, Captain Charles Mathews, P. Blake, Mr Veal, A. Yelland, -?-, Fred Nicholl, -?-.

Dennis Creek (c. 1897) in the foreground. The southernmost tip of today's built-up town is here being dammed off to provide access for the forthcoming railway.

Navvies working on the Iron Bridge in 1898. This was dangerous work, as shown by a newspaper article of June 18th 1898. "Shortly after dinner hour on Tuesday, while a gang of men were at work in a cutting at the rear of the newly built station, a heavy landslip happened, and before the men could get clear one of the trucks was forced from its position and imprisoned two navvies against the cliff on the side opposite to that where the landslip occurred. One of them extricated himself without difficulty and uninjured; the other, named Jackson and known as the 'General', was so tightly jammed between the wagon and the cliff that a portion of the wagon had to be cut away before the man could be got out. Drs Marley and Harvey were on the spot before Jackson was extricated and they examined him as soon as he was got out and again after he was carried to his lodgings. There are no bones broken but he is badly bruised about the abdomen and back; it is hoped there are no internal injuries. The news of the accident rapidly spread through the town and a big crowd gathered to watch the rescue."

Awaiting the first train, 23rd March 1899. The band and dignitaries are on the platform; members of the public at other vantage points.

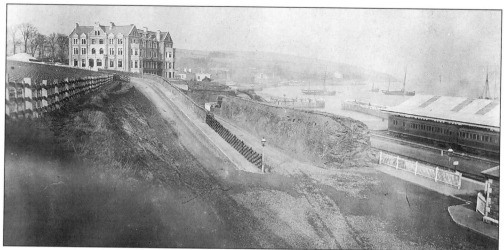

A view, c. 1905, of the South Western Hotel, showing the rock bluff through which Station Road was cut. In the background can be seen the fish dock and sheds.

The turntable, fish sheds and old fish quay about 1906. Here can clearly be seen the train that took the fish to London for the Billingsgate Market. The trains would pull up under the canopy, and the boxes and barrels of fish were loaded straight from the market into the train.

Lowestoft fishing vessels off Padstow, 1910. The vessel in the foreground is the smack *Research* LT1028 built in 1909. The quay is full of vessels other than those at anchor, evidence of the boom in the fishing industry during the early part of the century.

An early view of the station from the turntable. The little steamer on the right is the tug *Princess May*, which was used for towing the fishing smacks up river to the quay.

Padstow Station during the first quarter of the century. In the background is the burnt-out shell of Exbury House.

A view from above the station towards St Saviour's Point, c. 1904. In the ninety years since this photograph was taken the boatyard has been replaced by flats; the beach has been enclosed by the New Pier; the fields above the station have been built on; the two black sheds have gone; The Red Brick Building has been rebuilt; the Railway Dock has given way to the Dock; land has been reclaimed where the Harbour car park is sited, and, of course, the railway has gone.

An Adams 4-4-0 London and South Western Railway goods train on the sidings beside the fish quay 1909.

London and South Western Railway dock and shed in November 1909. At this time the Kipper House on the left has already been built. The identity of the ketch is unknown.

A view of the fish quay taken about 1904. Padstow's fishing industry boomed in the early 1900's resulting in the present Dock being built in 1912 to accommodate the fishing fleet.

Inside the Fish Market, looking through from the Dock towards the station. The boxes and barrels of fish are ready for loading into the goods train waiting under the canopy; a wagon can been seen behind Tom Tresidder, one of the station staff. Three of the fish merchants names can be identified on the containers: T. Mack Hyams, N. Hughes Plymouth and A. Goulden.

Padstow station staff, c. 1920. Back row: Will Martyn, George Edyvane, Tom Covill, Ernest Bennett, Jack Rattenbury, Charlie Blake. Front row: Tom Barratt, a relief from Exeter, Bill Coombes, Mr Stretch (the Station Master), Lew Kelland and Tom Tresidder.

By around 1920 the Bluff has gone, the Dock has been built, and land reclaimed where the present day Harbour Commissioners car park is sited.

London and South Western Railway engine number 636 and station staff at the fish sheds about 1914. Compared with the earlier photographs of the station, the number of tracks have increased and the Fish Market has been extended.

A view of the station signal box and fish sheds. In the background can be seen the Ice Factory. The Dock has been built in place of the old fish quay, dating the photograph to post 1912.

Padstow Station in the 1960's. The station and line were closed in 1967, the last train running to Wadebridge on the 28th January. Padstow was one of the lines hit by the Beeching reorganisation of 1964, the service gradually being reduced until eventual closure and the lifting of the track.

Four
Padstow: the Town

Men attending to the pulling lifeboat *Arab* at Cove, c. 1920. The Pilot Cottages in the background were built by the Padstow Harbour Commissioners and completed in 1874.

The Coastguard Station, c. 1910. The six pilots for the River Camel lived in the little cottages, and in December 1893 a dispute was reported by the *Western Morning News*. "Some of the men, night and day, had to be on watch for vessels entering the Harbour, and to pilot them in. These men in the pursuit of their duty had to, in the coldest weather, and heaviest gales, board their boats in the darkness of night. On occasions after rowing out in the roughest of weather they have been told, not always politely, that their services were not required, and they returned to their houses wet to the skin and benumbed with cold, for no financial gain. If the master of a vessel entering the Harbour reported to the authorities that no pilot was at his post, the man who should have been on watch is subject to dismissal, although it is optional whether the master of the vessel will engage his services. Padstow masters invariably embarked a pilot because they were acquainted with the hazardous and arduous duties pertaining to the pilotage of the Harbour." Now pilotage on specific types and size of vessel is compulsory, and the pilots are called when required by the Harbour Office.

Men and boys frolic in the water at Chidley Pumps, c. 1910.

Looking at the town from Stile, c. 1902. On the left of the path can be seen Mr Cowl's house and part of the boatyard with a ketch laying, perhaps for repair.

Men working in a boat yard on one of Captain Hutchings' vessels, believed to be the *Viola*. The exact location and names are unknown. A newspaper cutting of May 1892 relates an accident at one of the boatyards. "Mr William Henwood, a retired Trinity Pilot at Padstow, was yesterday morning engaged with several others in repairing and rigging the schooner *Courier*, and had himself rigged the shears for lifting the new mast onto her. As soon as the weight of the mast came upon the shears, they gave way, and fell upon him, crushing his both legs just above the foot. His left leg was amputated by Dr Griffin, and it is much feared that he will also lose his right leg."

The boatyard taken from Stile in the 1950's. Where a busy yard once stood are now blocks of flats obscuring the view from Stile – a blot on the appearance of the quay from all vantage points.

Fishing smacks tied up outside the harbour, c. 1910. Things were not always as calm as pictured here, as is shown by the following newspaper account. "A furious gale raged at Padstow on Tuesday night. Several Grimsby, Ramsgate, and Brixham steam and sailing trawlers were in the harbour and at anchor in the river. When the gale was at its height, several of these began to drag their anchors and their crews had a very exciting time in averting collisions and bringing the vessels to. Those of the crews who were on shore were unable to return to their vessels, as the wind lashed the sea into a fury, and no boat could venture off. At about 10p.m. the hooting of a steam trawler caused many people to assemble on the quays in spite of the downpour of rain. The Grimsby steam trawler *Goldfinder* and Ramsgate trawler No. 210 *Spitfire* were dragging badly and eventually both vessels went ashore under the ship yard on the North Beach. Immediately afterwards red flares were burnt on board a group of trawlers lying off the quay and of these the *Vanguard*, of Brixham, dragged her anchor and narrowly escaped collision, but more cable was payed out and the vessel held securely. At Hawker's Cove several steam trawlers were in difficulties with their anchors and the Trinity pilots and coastguards kept close watch on them. They were all securely moored in the cove without accident. On Wednesday morning the *Goldfinder* and the *Spitfire* were got off the beach having sustained no serious damage."

Padstow, 136

The Lower Beach, c. 1910, where Lowestoft smacks await the tide. The vessel in the foreground is the *Kathleen*, registration number LT 1073.

Scottish steam herring drifters on the beach, c. 1911. The vessels are INS313 *Roosevelt*, PD239 *City of Hull*, BF877 *Jeanie Gilchrist*, INS174 *Caledonia* and INS401 *Glengynack*.

Steam trawlers berthed on Langford's Quay, c. 1920. The photograph is taken from the Lower Beach, which appears to be shillet with no evidence of the present day mud.

Langford's Quay, c. 1930. The *Elizabeth*, which brought stone from Stepper Point Quarry, gets ready to discharge onto a waiting lorry. The other little ketch is the *Bonita*.

Langford's Quay, c. 1910. It appears that a fair is setting up on the quay. The Brixham sailing smack registration BM141 is the *Smiling Morn*.

The Quay, c. 1927. The sailing vessels on the North Wall are the *Gypsy Maid* inside of the *Lord Devon*. The other two large vessels are *FCT* on the left and the *Lady Ann Mandall*. The long cutter is Bill England's *Our Boys*. In the foreground is Jimmy Morrissey graining bulwarks; the white punt astern is *Marjorie*, with Bob England and his punt alongside. The other vessels are the *Kingfisher*, *Annie Kate*, *Sea Mills Lass* and the barge *Grand Turk* on the right hand edge.

Lowestoft fishing vessels moored in the quay, c. 1910. The vessels are, from left to right: *Pet* LT.560 (owner J. Breach), *Comrades* LT.990 (owner G. Catchpole), *Inverna* LT.514 (owner C.H. Crews), *Inverlyon* LT.687 (owner W.J. Williams Jnr) and *Waverley* LT.464 (owner W.J. Williams).

Fishing smacks in the quay, c. 1910. The bowsprits are all drawn in while moored.

The North Quay, c. 1927. The *Adele* PW3 was built in Yarmouth in 1915 and was Padstow's only steam trawler; Bill Gamble was skipper and Sheri Constance engineer.

The old Long Lugger and West Quay before the Cory Memorial Shelter was built in 1932. Mr Dawe's boot and shoe repair shop can just be seen through the rigging of the ship.

Mr and Mrs John Appleton in the garden of their house, where the Cory Memorial Shelter now stands. Mr Thomas Henry Williams said of this house, "Probably one of the oldest buildings in Padstow, of Queen Elizabeth I period. Seawater floated the chairs on spring tides. On taking down the house we found old ships' cabin beams with gold leaf on the moulds as good as the day they were done. Also found, *War Cry* magazines dated 18?? in the name of Mr Penalegan."

The West Quay, c. 1905, not recognisable as the West Quay of today. The two barges are the *Grand Turk* and the *Marco Polo*.

The Strand and South Quay, c. 1905. Next to the ketch is a barge. Barges were in frequent use in Padstow for transporting slate and stone from Stepper Quarry and, amongst other produce, corn, coal and sand between Wadebridge, Rock and Padstow. A barge manned by N. England and W. Prior, carrying road stone from Stepper Quarry to Padstow Quay for the use of the Padstow Urban District Council, got into difficulties and sank in deep water at the Narrows. The men took to their boat, which was drawn under by the sinking vessel, and were thrown into the sea. The coastguard at Hawker's Cove saw what was happening and the men were rescued by the coastguard gig and lifeboat *Helen Peele*; the barge was a total loss.

A busy scene; smart pedestrians stroll past Bray's shop and Henwood's stores. Note the gas light on the corner. Padstow's gas lighting was a bone of contention, as can be seen from this cutting of 18th October 1887: "After half past seven on Sunday evening Padstow was left in darkness, the public lamps, on account of an insufficient supply of gas, having been extinguished at that hour. Owing to the absence of light, a gentleman who was returning to his residence at ten o'clock walked over the quay and fell a depth of 15 feet, but the tide being out, he landed on the soft sea mud with which the basin is well filled and so escaped without injury. The price of gas at Padstow being 7s. 6d. per thousand (therms), the highest price, it is said, paid in the kingdom, the strictest economy possible is practised in the use of the illuminant with regard to the street lamps, private houses, and public buildings, as it is felt that a good light by such a costly method is a luxury in which only the well-to-do can indulge."

The steamer *Collier* lying alongside of the railway berth. LSWR goods trucks are on the quay behind the vessel. This steamer plied between Bristol, Swansea, Ilfracombe and Padstow. A newspaper of 10th March 1891 reported a "Cranky Character" who, wearing grand apparel, kid gloves and a massive gold albert watch, boarded the vessel without any luggage. The Captain asked the gentleman courteously for his fare. He regarded the Captain's question as impertinent and, on being asked again quietly, said he had no money; this reply aroused the ire of the Captain, who was personally responsible for the fare. On some oaths and threats being shouted, the man began to shake violently, and to the delight of the passengers, sixpences and threepenny pieces began to fall from his suit onto the deck. This man went on to St Merryn where he outstayed the local hospitality and ended up being chased away by two men with hay-forks.

Padstow between 1860 and 1870. On the far left is the boatyard and shed which was on the site of the present council offices and station car park. The long row of cottages is Avery's Row, with St Edmund's house at the top, and the building which preceded the Memorial Hall at the bottom. In front of them on the water's edge are the boatyard sheds and the Drill Shed used by the Artillery. To the right is Court House, which was shortened on the coming of the railway. Next to the Court House are the Riverside Cottages which abut onto the Custom House, whose gig hangs on davits on its front. To the right of the Custom House is a row of cottages. In the foreground are the tops of the buildings used by the saw pit on the North Quay.

The South Quay, c. 1885. Here can clearly be seen the Higher Yard. Compare the shape of the yard's outside wall to the reclaimed land of the railway station in the next photograph. The old wall of the boatyard has obviously been used to contain the infill. The warehouse has now been built on the corner of the South Quay, and next to it is an old cottage. Court House is still in its original form prior to being cut back to the second doorway.

56

Padstow, c. 1905. Here can clearly be seen the LSWR Dock and the station which has been built since the previous photograph. The cliff face behind the station has been dramatically blasted out; Court House has been shortened; the sheds in front of the present day Memorial Hall are gone; the Hotel Metropole, then called the South Western Hotel, has been built. Next to the Custom House, some of the Riverside Cottages have been replaced by two red brick houses, and the cottage in Strand Street has been demolished and replaced by a longer building.

A summer day on the quay by the Custom House Slip, c. 1908.

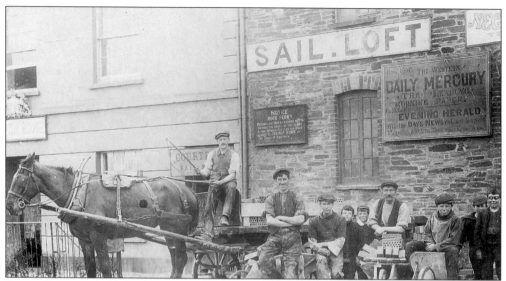

Riverside, c. 1912. The wagon appears to be carrying bricks, presumably to build the red brick houses to the south of the CustomHouse. The identities of the boys are unknown, but the man driving the wagon is believed to be a Phillips; to his left are Archie Gard, Bill Giddy, and Alf Davey. Behind these men on the wall are signs for the Courtenay brothers sail loft and Joshua Rawe's ferry.

The Quay, c. 1910. Men congregated around the quay, which proved lucky for Master Robert Chapman, as can be seen from this newspaper account of 28th August 1898. "Robert Chapman, aged about eight years of age, son of Captain R. Chapman, was sculling a boat in Padstow Harbour yesterday, when the oar slipped, and the little fellow fell into the water and sank. The accident was seen by Mr B.M. Harvey, who, without divesting himself of his clothes or watch, pluckily sprung into the water with the intention of rescuing the drowning boy, but before he reached him the lad was picked up by Mr Andrew Crenells, who got into a boat moored near the place where the boy fell overboard."

The Quay, c. 1927. The ketches moored in the centre of the quay are the *FCT* and *Mary Ann Mandall*. Two Lowestoft steam trawlers are berthed on the Railway Quay; the one nearest the camera is LT.1124, the *EWB*, built in 1911 and owned by the Viking Steam Fishing Co. Ltd.

The site of the Padstow Harbour Commissioners' South Quay car park, c. 1925. In the foreground are coal yards. Padstow's coal porters were in dispute at the time of this newspaper cutting of 13th May 1890. "Padstow coal porters are demanding of the coal merchants an increase in pay. Up to the present they have been paid at the rate of $1\frac{1}{4}$d. per ton per man for discharging coals, but they have recently become dissatisfied with this amount, and yesterday morning several notices, of which the following is a copy, were posted around the quays. 'Notice. 12th May 1890. We, the undersigned, beg to inform the coal merchants of Padstow that in future we demand three-halfpence per ton for discharging coals. Hoping that you will concede to our moderate demand, we remain, yours obediently, R. Thomas, W. Parish, H. Brenter, T. Nugent, G. Phillips, J. Brabyn, S. Daniel, J. Flee, S. Henwood, M. Bate, T. Pollard, W. Smith, R. Jay, James Stone, John Stone, J. Brunyee, H. McEwan, G. Edyvane, J. Phillips, J. Daly, J. Bate, R. Brenter, W. Crews, P. Keefe, W. Minney, S. Bate, W. Jermyn.'"

The Fishmarket, c. 1905. The market, then an open building, looks to be busy with boxes and baskets piled high, and fishermen and merchants bustling about. Behind the market can be seen one of the trains that took the fish to London.

Padstow to Rock ferry at Rock, c. 1912. This vessel appears to be a little motor boat; earlier, Padstow had a steam ferry. A letter regarding this ferry appears in the *Western Morning News* of 8th April 1885. "In consequence of a report appearing under the heading of West of England news in your issue of Thursday last that 'a coach would be conveyed from Padstow to Rock and back by the above ferry on the Bank Holiday' many persons on both sides of the river were on the lookout at the time named for the event to take place. Allow me to state that the directors are not responsible for the report, and they are very sorry that the public should have been misled. There is no necessity to prove that a coach can be taken across the river in safety, weather permitting, as last season, among many other vehicles, a wagonette and pair and a wagon loaded with furniture were safely conveyed across. The many puffing and misleading paragraphs that have appeared from time to time in your paper have seriously interfered with the successful carrying out of an undertaking which is undoubtedly of great benefit to the district.

The Strand, c. 1920. Lack of pavements gives the narrow street a feeling of spaciousness.

Dickie Brenton surrounded by children in Edwardian dress poses for his photograph to be taken in the Market Place, c. 1916.

The Market, c. 1895. In the background, on the site of the present Barclays Bank, is the old Post Office, which ten years earlier had been renovated, as illustrated by this newspaper cutting of 17th December 1885. "For the last fifteen years the accommodation afforded by the Padstow Post Office has been of the most circumscribed nature, and great inconvenience has thus been caused. The counter at which stamps were sold, telegrams written, deposits for the savings bank received, Post Office and postal orders, and dog and gun licenses issued, was about two feet by 18 inches in extent, and the standing room for the customers waiting their turn was a passage about six feet in length by two and half in width, so that it often happened just before the closing of the mail in the afternoon, when four or five persons of both sexes were gathered in this narrow place, that those who were in the inside had the utmost difficulty in making their exit, unless they were the very leanest of lean kind. Then again, everyone present was, willingly or unwillingly, made cognisant of the business of the others. Within the last few days, however, a great change has taken place. The partition between the office and the room adjoining has been removed, and the result is, that, for a small town, a large and commodious office has been provided, with the accommodation for all business purposes, which contrasts most favourably with the office which has done duty for so many years, and there are now afforded opportunities for transacting business without all the other persons present being aware of what is being done...." At the same time the sub-postmaster Mr W. Brown handed over to his daughter MissBrown.

A view across the town, c. 1860. Tredwen Court in Middle Street has not yet been built, nor has Oak Terrace. In St Saviour's Lane (below the ink blob) is a round summer house which was used by the Prideaux Brune family.

The Market, c. 1937, showing Hicks & Capell where the Midland Bank now stands, G. May Jeweller, since replaced by Barclays Bank, E.C. Williams, Newsagent and W.M. Prior, Barber. The advert is for Popes Café, which was to the left of the entrance to the Cinedrome. Edgar Pope was the original proprietor of the Cinedrome, Café and Emporium, which was on the opposite corner of Middle Street.

Looking from the Quay towards Mill Square. The old mill building is now the Flower Shop. The Mill Leat, which ran from the church down Duke Street and behind the Old Ship, caused problems in bad weather as shown in this newspaper article of 13th December 1893. "Throughout Monday night and yesterday morning the wind blew with hurricane force, constantly veering from point to point. Rain commenced to fall about ten o'clock on Monday night and continued until midday. During the night the flashes of lightning were very frequent and exceptionally vivid. The rain fell in one steady and copious downpour and very few houses in the town proved waterproof. The Mill Leat which runs through the main sewers from the upper part of the town proved incapable of carrying off such an unusual rush of water and many houses under which or near which it flows were inundated. Some of the drains at the lower part of the town were choked and the streets, where level, were one sheet of water, and where sloping were covered with a rushing river. About noon the rain ceased, and the sun shone forth brightly."

Henwood's Mill at the bottom of Little Hill. Thomas Henwood, Wine and Spirit Merchant, brewed his own beer. The family still have an off-licence of this name on the quay, run by direct descendants.

Church Street, c. 1910. A cat sits in the doorway by the cobbled pavement.

An aerial view of New Street, c. 1920, showing the school with its bell tower; the allotments opposite are all tealed; above the school are fields on which Caswarth Terrace now stands.

An aerial view of the town, c. 1920, looking down Church Street and Duke Street towards the Quay. The New Pier was not built at this time.

Prideaux Place on a sunny Whitsun afternoon. The grounds are opened to the locals, who congregate and socialize in their Sunday best.

The Pioneer, which ran between Padstow, Boscastle, St Columb and Newquay. Locally these vehicles were called "buses". In 1887 the *Western Morning News* reported that Mr Badgery, being unable to turn a bus he was driving in Mrs Foley's Square, decided to reach the yard via the quay. As the horses went around the quay they were alarmed by some chains used for mooring vessels. The driver lost control of the animals and they backed over the quay, falling into the mud. The driver managed to jump clear, but his wife who was sitting in the box seat was carried over with the bus. Mr Hambly, a pedestrian, was knocked over by one of the wheels. Neither the man or woman were injured but one of the horses had a badly cut neck. The bus was almost unharmed, but attempts to extricate it from the mud proved disastrous and the bus, once back on dry land, was a total wreck.

Netherton Road before the council houses were built.

Mr and Mrs Fuller in Commercial Court, c. 1966. These cottages were knocked down and similar buildings substituted. Note the gate, hanging on the gatepost by the stone steps, which enclosed the courtyard of the pub.

The Morning Star, Padstow's sanitary cart. This was a gimbled barrel on an axle. Dr Blaxall's report to the local board with reference to the Typhoid epidemic of 1876 states under the heading Excrement Removal and Disposal. "The means employed for excrement removal and disposal consists of pails, pan-closets, and cesspit privies. The pails were introduced with a view to meet the difficulty experienced in providing privy accommodation for such of the dwellings as had no ground space attached, but they have been extended to houses where no such obstacle exists; they resemble ordinary slop-pails with covers and are made use of to receive the contents of the chamber utensils. The pails are obliged to stand in occupied rooms or in the immediate vicinity of the dwellings, but they appear to be kept in a cleanly condition, and to be occasionally used for general purposes. No means of deodorization are employed. Each morning the pails are placed outside the doors of the dwellings when a scavenger calls round with a large wooden tub, into which he empties the contents and carts them away into the country, where they are stored for agricultural purposes. The process of removal is much complained of as creating nuisance, and apparently not without cause, as the wooden tub above referred to was at the time of my visit saturated with filth, showing that the cleansing of it is greatly neglected, although disinfectants are said to be provided for the purpose."

Five
May and Merriment

The Circus comes to Town. An elephant at the bottom of Strand Street in the 1920's. Apparently the circus tent was pitched in the triangular field where the road splits to Padstow and Trecerus, coming from Treator. The elephants were brought to the quay for a "paddle".

Queen Victoria's Golden Jubilee celebrations were described in a newspaper article of 23rd June 1887. "In splendid weather, the Queen's jubilee was celebrated on Tuesday according to programme, and was carried out in all its various parts in good spirit. Arches, evergreens, and bunting were conspicuous about the town and on the shipping in the harbour. The church bells were rung merrily at intervals through the day. At eleven o'clock a service was held in the church, which was largely attended by the general public and the children of the Church and Wesleyan Sunday schools, the service commencing with the National Anthem, all the children being provided with a copy. The order of service appointed by the Archbishop was used. The Revs. J. Murley (vicar of St Merryn) and John Daunt (curate of Padstow) officiated. Hymns A&M Nos. 165, 166, service concluding with a repetition of the National Anthem. At 2p.m. a luncheon was partaken of by several hundreds of the inhabitants, of whom 350 were by free tickets, the tables extending from the Market-place up through the Broad Street, the same tables being utilised for the childrens free tea at 5p.m., of which many hundreds partook. Afterwards there was a tea for the general public, this also being well attended. The young minstrels band of music enlivened the proceedings through the day. In the evening a fire balloon was sent up from the Broad Street by Mr E. Griffith, followed by a display of fireworks. The principal attractions of the evening was the march (headed by the band and the committee) to the locality of the bonfire at Crugmeer Cross, the highest ground in the parish, where many hundreds of persons assembled and saw no less than thirty or more bonfires. There was a discharge of cannon and a dance near the bonfire, when the party returned to town highly pleased with the day's proceedings.

The brass band lead a Whitsuntide Church parade into the Lawn, c. 1890. The large crowd marching up New Street carry banners and flags, flags are also decorating the highway. Note the changes that have taken place over the last century: the road has been widened and pavements put in; the old barn on the right has been cut back and turned into a dwelling with a conservatory on the back, and the old wall and gate which led to the Drill Hall have gone, as have most of the old walls on the left. A garage has been built abutting the topmost cottage on the left, and on the opposite side of the road the old garages have been demolished and new cottages built in their place.

The band lead a Wesleyan Whitsuntide parade down Duke Street, c. 1912. Behind the band can been seen the children waving their flags; all the children were given flags to wave.

Bray and Parkyn's wagon decorated for a carnival in the early 1940's. On the cart, dressed as footballers, are Bobby Blackwell (standing), Trevor Fuller (sitting below him), Stella Plowman, with the blond curly hair, Neil Burke, -?-, Glanville Hope, Brenda Hope (sitting holding the ball), Michael Hornabrook, Joey Bate (above him), and, below them, Stan Key, Jimmy Tregembo, Roy Plowman and Edward Puddiphatt. The identity of the driver is unknown; Phillip "Chuggy" May is at the front of the cart.

The Sansoni Acrobatic Troupe. The sign at the back of the wagon says Bennetto's Acrobats. Ham and Jenden's bakers shop can be seen in the background. The wagon is probably part of a parade or carnival in the 1920's on its way up to Punnion.

74

Sunday School FÊTE.
Padstow. May 1920.

Padstow Sunday School Fête at Trethillick sports field in May 1920. The umbrellas are out so the weather must have been poor, though it doesn't seem to have put a damper on the busy scene.

St Merryn School's production of *Uncle Tom Cobleigh and All*. Details of boys and date are unknown.

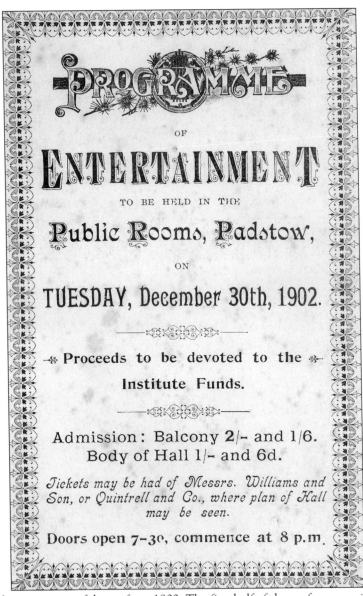

PROGRAMME

OF

ENTERTAINMENT

TO BE HELD IN THE

Public Rooms, Padstow,

ON

TUESDAY, December 30th, 1902.

Proceeds to be devoted to the

Institute Funds.

**Admission: Balcony 2/- and 1/6.
Body of Hall 1/- and 6d.**

Tickets may be had of Messrs. Williams and Son, or Quintrell and Co., where plan of Hall may be seen.

Doors open 7-30, commence at 8 p.m.

The front of a programme of drama from 1902. The first half of the performance is a piano duet by Miss Nicholls and Mr F.B. Harvey, and songs by Annie Foley, J. Clemow, J. Hawken, J. Lobb, Mrs Hoore and Mrs Langford. The second half is a costume farce entitled *Ticklish Times*, set in Weymouth in 1750, the cast being Mr H.J. and L. Lobb, Miss W. Lobb, Mr F.B. Harvey, Mr W. Brown and Miss J. Foley. The Public Rooms, which many will know as the old Fire Station, stood opposite Barry's Lane and was at one time used by many local groups. On Whit-Wednesday 1877 an unfortunate dispute took place between the male officers and teachers of the Wesleyan Sunday School and the Teetotal Executive. The Wesleyans contended that they could use the rooms without applying for permission, the teetotallers saying they could only "save" on Sundays. The Sunday School Teachers refused to make a written application for the room but, proceeding to extreme measures, mustered their strength and broke open the gate and door of the rooms and so obtained access. In the scene that ensued tables were overturned and opprobrious epithets were freely indulged in.

Some of the cast of St Merryn Musical Society's *Babes in the Wood*. The play was written and produced by Jack Ingrey. After being shown at St Merryn, the company would then go on tour to St Columb and Wadebridge Town Halls. Will Scarlet: Dora Bray; Ned: Ken Smith; Prunella: Ruth Allen; Little John: Charles Pitman; Robin Hood: Jean Curtis; Maid Marion: Mary Burke; Little Nell: Trixie Cowling; Blackfoot Indian White Eagle: Bill Cheyney; Flame Goddess: Jean Bennett; Blackfoot Indian Sitting Bull: Ken Gray.

The cast of *Aladdin*, performed by the St Merryn Musical Society, 2nd to 14th January 1956, written and produced by Jack Ingrey. Back row: "Curley" Allen, Colin Cleave, Donald Weekes, Neil Burke, Jack Ingrey, Jim Harper, Leonard Buscombe, Albert Dadswell, Ernest Angell, Anthony Angell, Ken Gray, Olive Dadswell. Front row: Marjorie Reynolds, Louvaine Newcombe, Esther Trenouth, Annie Newcombe, Rita Adams, Joy Dingle, Percy Keast, Ken Smith, Elsie Gray, Alex Bray.

Mrs Singer's Orchestra, c. 1946. Jack Thomas (accordion), Bob Beare (bass), Jean Carhart (accordion), Douglas Smith (drums), Anita Singer (vocalist), Gerald Carhart (trumpet and sax), Mrs Singer (piano).

King and Queen of the Fairies at Padstow Sunday School, 1933. Edna Bate, Eric Champion, Dorothy Jermyn, Freddie Disburry, -?- (behind him), Phyllis Horn, Violet Dale, Jean Fuller and Aileen Cruise.

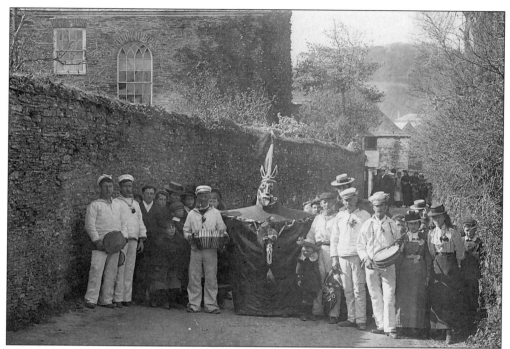

The 'Oss in Dennis Road in the early part of the century. With tambourines: Charlie "Shackles" Bate and Mac McOwen. Sam England is next to them. To the left of the 'Oss is "Bluey" England with the melodeon. Far right with the drum is Jimmy "Wiggy" Stone. The other Mayers in the photograph are unidentified. Note the teazers mask being held to the right of the 'Oss.

May Day, c. 1920. William Thomas in the fancy jacket, Sam England in the sailor suit, Percy Baker wearing the black arm band, Jack Brenton is behind the 'Oss and "Bluey" England with drum.

May Day, c. 1923. A large crowd watches the Old 'Oss cavorting around the Maypole.

May Day, late 1920's. Albert Dale, Mr Giddy, Mr Gamble, -?-, Kathleen Humphries, Pat or Glynn O'Keefe, Mrs Plowman, Mrs O'Keefe, Mary Thomas, Jim Tonkyn, Bubbles Phillips, Sam Phillips. In the foreground are Marjorie Magor and Bill Thomas with the club.

At the back are Jack England (with melodeon), Randall Jermyn, Annie Bate, Willie McOwen (with drum), Mildred Gregor, Dick Gregor (in her arms), Will Giddy, Mrs Bishop, Miss Williams, Ernie Bate. In the front are "Chum" Kane, Beattie Bate, Ron Leverton, George Bate (with the club) and Ron Stone.

A childrens 'Oss and group in the Strand, c. 1931. Betty Cribbens, Jim Hawke (with the tambourine), Charles "Brown" Cribbens, -?-, Tom Lobb (with the club), Sidney Aunger (with the drum), Sam Lobb, Gill Lobb. At the back are Randall Jermyn, Lily Jermyn and Mick Chegwidden.

May Day, c. 1937. Brooke Buckingham with club, John Murt with melodeon, Sedwin Wills and Tony Magor with the drum.

The Peace 'Oss in the Market, c. 1931. In the foreground, to the left of the 'Oss, is Reg Gill, and to its right Harry Brenton. The other people are, from left to right: Betty Clark, Elsie Edwards, Jack Phillips, Clifford Hill, -?-, Albert Dale, Cashie Murt, Derek Grubb, Gerald Dawe, Muriel Hornabrook, Ed O'Keefe, -?-, Carrie Williams, Reg Underhill, Sam Phillips, Randall Jermyn, George Brenton, Albert Giddy, George Bate, Victor Cullum, Kenneth Champion, Joe Apps.

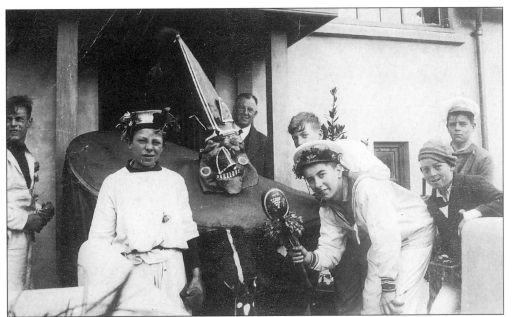

Outside Mr Carkeet's, May 1st 1935. Ron Crews, Edgar Fuller, George Martyn in the 'Oss, Mr Carkeet, Bobby Dale with the club, -?-, Wilfred Leverton and Sidney Aunger.

Recording the May Song, May 1st 1936. From left to right: Mrs Smith and daughter Joyce, Betty Fuller, Carrie Williams, Owen Curtis (standing with the drum), -?-, Sam Martyn, Dick Gregor (the boy at the back), Jinny May, Tom Gregor, Jack McOwen (the harlequin), Olive Chidgey, Jack Brenton, Mary O'Keefe. In the front are Tom Stone (with the drum), Harry Bate, Tom Pepler (with the banjo), Bill Gard (with the club) and Walter "Colonel" Bate with the collecting tin.

Harvey May wearing the Peace 'Oss teazer's mask, c. 1948.

Fred Lawrence with the Peace 'Oss in the Market, c. 1939.

The Old 'Oss Party in the Stable at the Golden Lion, c. 1952 . Back row: Charlie Bate, Tom Jasper Snr, George Giddy, Bill Gard, Tom Stone, Willie McOwen, Roderick Rosevear, Tom Gard, Ernie Bate, Owen Curtis, Tom Jasper. Front row: George Giddy, Tom Bate, Walter Bate, Micky Bate, Jack McOwen, Tommy Gregor, Mrs Couch, Laurie Giddy.

Six

Harvest Time

Three horses pull the binder at Polmark Farm, St Merryn. The binder was a machine for harvesting corn: a knife in front of the binder would automatically cut the corn which would be pulled onto a canvas belt by the windmill-like arms called reels. When on the canvas it was bundled up and tied with binder twine to make sheaves, prior to being distributed in piles on the field.

Trehembourne Farm, c. 1914. John Bennett can be seen on the far left leaning against the traction engine's water cart; to his left, Tremain Bennett stands at the back of the traction engine, which was used to drive the threshing machine. Behind the cart and engine can be seen the rick which contained the sheaves of corn to be threshed. These would be thrown to the men on the top platform of the threshing machine; one would have a penknife to cut the binder twine which held the sheaf together, the other man would tend him. The corn would then be put into a large rotating drum on top of the machine which would do the threshing. At the back of the machine can be seen the elevator which lifted the bundles of straw to the top of the newly formed rick; from the other end of the machine came the grain, which was automatically graded and poured into West of England sacks which weighed $1\frac{1}{4}$ cwt when full. The waste product was called "doust". Mrs Susan Bennett can be seen sitting on one of the West of England sacks on the right.

Threshing at Trethillick Farm, Padstow. These men can be seen tending to the West of England sacks. The sacks were placed on hooks into which the grain was poured.

Harvestime at the farm

Threshing at Crigmorrick, St Merryn. On the left is the traction engine, with a belt driving the threshing machine, and far right the elevator being adjusted by guide ropes. The set, or threshing machine, traction engine and elevator, would not normally be owned by one farmer but by a contractor who would be contracted to attend with his gang and to thresh the farmers corn. At least twelve men were required during threshing, some being provided by the farmer, some by the contractor.

Threshing at Slight's Farm, Tregirls, Padstow, c. 1920. The belt providing the power from the traction engine can be seen on the right of the picture.

Threshing the corn at Polmark Farm, St Merryn. This threshing machine was owned and run by Alfie and Billy Wilcox. On top of the machine, and bending over, is Derek Cripps. The cart on the left with iron wheels is the water cart for the engine.

A happy scene. The harvesters at Polmark Farm, St Merryn have "crib", c. 1930. The adults are, from left to right: Mr Joe Ball, the farm owner (in the white hat), Trevor Williams and Mrs Brenton, at the back, Dorothy Sluman, in the front with Cyril Ball, Mrs Ball, behind them, and above her, an unidentified old lady, then Miss Brenton, Harold Ball and Mrs Janie Howe.

Binding at Trevethan Farm, Porthcothan, c. 1930. The *Western Morning News* of 20th July 1892 reported: "Mr Thomas Henwood, Casworth Farm, Padstow, cut a field of winter oats on Monday, and the occasion was chosen to give the 'Mercier' binder its first trial in England. At the invitation of Mr J.P. Tom Dennis, agent for the machine, a large number of agriculturists were present to see the machine at work. The crop of oats was a heavy one and most difficult to harvest. Notwithstanding this, the machine did its work in a way that elicited from all the practical gentlemen present unstinted praise.... Considering that it is a new machine, it was thought to be light in draught, and being constructed without canvas it is not liable to be put out of gear by rain or dew as all of the old style of machines are...."

A view of a binder from behind. The sheaves of corn would fall down the canvas and be collected on the tynes visible on the right of the binder. When four or five sheaves were laying on the tynes the sheaves were ejected from the machine in a pile to make it easier for the sheaves to be collected for building shocks. This binder is working Polmark Farm, St Merryn.

Cyril Ball oiling the binder at Polmark Farm, St Merryn. in the background are sheaves of corn piled up into shocks.

After the binder had cut and bundled up the corn into sheaves, the sheaves would be built into wigwam-shaped structures called shocks. One shock would have about nine sheaves arranged in such a manner that they supported each other. In the background can be seen the binder working one of the fields of Lellizzick Farm, Padstow.

In the photograph on the left the sheaves of corn are put onto a hay wagon using pikes or pronged forks. Mr Joe Ball is on top of the wagon and his son Harold at the back. The photograph on the right shows Mr Ball taking the sheaves by wagon to the mowhay for building into a corn rick.

Here the hay wagon is ready for loading. This hard though harmless task almost spelled disaster for one young man, as reported in a paper of 24th July 1882. "Practical joking has resulted seriously at Padstow. Richard Nance, a man whose intellect is not of the brightest, was engaged with others on the Trevone Estate, Padstow, carrying hay, when some boys entered the field and bound him round over the arms with a rope fastened to a wagon. The horses in the wagon galloped off, either from their own accord or were purposely driven, and drew Nance at the tail of the wagon. The strain caused the rope to slip over the shoulders to his neck, and when the horses stopped the affair which had been considered as a good joke, was found to be a very serious matte,r for 'Dicky', as Nance is familiarly called, was found to be very nearly dead. He was ill for several hours, but gradually recovered."

Lellizzick Farm. Sheaves of corn from the shocks are being piked onto the wagon for transportation back to the mowhay, the mowhay being the stackyard or rickyard.

Building a corn rick at Tredore Farm. The sheaves which have been brought from the field to the mowhay are formed into a rick which will be thatched with straw to keep the rain out. The corn will be left as a rick until it is threshed.

A hay rake at Polmark Farm, St Merryn, c. 1932. After the field had been cleared of shocks of corn the hay rake would then go around the field to pick up any useful material. These rakings would be used as animal fodder and bedding. On the left is Mr Joe Ball, with his horse Diamond; on the seat of the rake is his son Cyril. His other son, Harold, is standing by the wheel.

Rev. Jones conducts the Harvest Festival Service in the Chapel which is now the Masonic Hall in Ruthy's Lane, Padstow.

Harvest festival in St Merryn Sunday School Hall, c. 1930. A newspaper report of 19th September 1889 states: "Harvest festivities in St Merryn concluded with a very successful concert given in the Sunday Schoolroom, the proceeds of which, together with the receipts from the services, the public tea and sale of work, were devoted to the Restoration Fund of the parish church, upon which a heavy debt still exists...." The report continues, giving the details of performers in the concert.

Mr and Mrs Leslie Hawken, landlord and landlady of the Cornish Arms, St Merryn, proudly pose for a photograph in the lounge bar which has been decorated for a harvest festival service and sale.

Seven

St Merryn and Environs

The Davis family pose for a family photograph outside of their house at Trevear, St Merryn. Behind them is the farmhouse that stood on the bank and was demolished in the 1930's. In this picture, taken c. 1897, are: Chrissie, Thomas Henry (the father), Louise (the mother), Annie, Dick, Dora, Amy, Hilda May (later Babs Bennett) and Katie.

Farm labourers' cottages, which stood on the bank at Trevear, St Merryn, to the rear of the now demolished farmhouse which could be seen behind the Davis family in the photograph on page 95. These have long since disappeared. It is hard to imagine how one could raise a family in such a small house, with few comforts. My great-great-great-grandparents John and Elizabeth May, who had ten children, lived in one of these little cottages.

The back of the large cottages at Trevear, St Merryn. On the opposite side of the road is an orchard. Today these cottages have been modernised.

Trehembourne Farmhouse, St Merryn, c. 1910. This is a view across the meadow to the front and side of the house. At the bottom of the picture is the old mill pond, which during the past sixty years has silted up. This farm was owned by the Champion family until, early in the twentieth century, the Hicks family from St Wenn bought it. They still farm it.

Outside of Rose Cottage, Trehembourne, St Merryn, c. 1920. Mrs Beatrice Carne, the occupier of the cottage, posed for this photograph with Mrs Flewitt. The cottage in the background with the gable end to the road was once a chapel.

Towan Green, St Merryn, c. 1900. This quaint scene is still recognisable if you look hard; many of the buildings have been renovated and changed from barns to private residences. The farmhouse on the left was for many years occupied by the Andrew family.

Higher Trevorgus Farmhouse, St Merryn, c. 1900. The Strongman family, who worked the farm, are standing beside their front porch.

Postman Joe Brown, with his wicker post cart, outside of the old post office, St Merryn, c. 1920. Mr Brown delivered the mail for Padstow, then pushed his trolley to St Merryn to deliver their mail, calling on all the farms on the way. Once the St Merryn post was delivered, he would leave his trolley, don a basket and then deliver the St Eval post. Apparently, Mr Brown did not walk – he trotted!

The new post office, St Merryn, c. 1925. Far left is the Farmers Arms, and between the pub and new post office may be seen an old cottage, the former post office. The old post office building was demolished and Lyndale built in its place in 1939. Lyndale was built to match its neighbouring building.

St Merryn Garage, c. 1929. This garage on St Merryn crossroads was built and run by Mr Henry Gridley, uncle to the present owner John Ball. It was not unusual for the local blacksmith to open the first garage in the village; here it was Mrs Gridley's grandfather, Mr Lobb, who was the local blacksmith.

St Merryn Churchtown at the turn of the century. On the right is Treveglos Farm, with outbuildings on the opposite side of the road. The church is distinctive, top centre, making this location easily identifiable.

RULES

OF

ST. MERRYN PIG CLUB,

JULY, 1887.

1. That the club shall consist of an unlimited number of Members, also that the Society shall not be broken up nor the stock divided so long as any ten Members are willing to support the same; and if any member or members shall otherwise propose, he or they shall forfeit the sum of two shillings, and on refusing to pay the same shall be excluded the society.

2. That there be four stewards chosen annually out of the members for the purpose of collecting subscriptions and fines, visiting and deciding in cases of sick pigs, and marking all pigs belonging to the club; and that each member shall be at the risk of his pig until he give notice to the nearest Steward of marking the same, either personally or in writing; and should the said steward neglect to mark the aforesaid pig within five days, he shall be fined the sum of one shilling; and should the said member neglect to enforce the fine on the steward, if proved, he shall also be fined the same as the steward. Should any member have more than two pigs marked in one year, he shall pay two-pence to the steward for marking each of the others, also the fines so collected to be paid over immediately to the Treasurer.

3. That each member shall pay or cause to be paid on the first Tuesday after every quarter day the sum of six-pence, or be fined the sum of three-pence, to be paid to the steward appointed for that purpose, at such time and place as the said steward shall direct, and if such fines and subscriptions be not paid up by the next collecting day, the member so neglecting shall be excluded.

4. That any member lately losing his pig, shall within ten days after the sum being affixed, receive of the treasurer the price to be awarded at one farthing under the butchers' buying price, and to be at the whole weight of his pig; and if in cases of sick pigs any member shall kill his pig before finding any disease, or giving notice to the stewards, and afterwards there should be a failure, except pease shall in no case receive any benefit, and in case of pease the loss to be decided by the stewards, and in case where stewards are called they shall immediately proceed to value the pig, and so on as called on, and if the pig should recover, the four stewards shall decide on the loss, and in default of any steward or stewards neglecting their duty, unless prevented by sickness or extreme necessity, and then to send their key by one of the members to act in their behalf; and not to be later than seven o'clock every quarter night, shall be fined six-pence, and default of payment to be excluded.

5. That any member shall dispose of his interest in the club to any person the majority of the club may approve of, but the party so becoming a member shall not come to the full benefit of the club for the space of three months after, and in case of the death of a member his interest shall descend to the Widow or Children if approved of.

6. That if any new member wishes to join the society may at any quarter meeting by paying two shillings and sixpence entering money, and risk his pig three months, and pay his quarterage regularly so long as until an accident should occur, when all the members will again advance their quarter arrears, and then to be free as the standing members.

7. That any member refusing to serve in the office of a steward after being duly elected, or neglecting his duty shall be fined the sum of one shilling, the fines to be paid the same in this case as in rule the fourth, and no substitute allowed.

8. That in case of the sudden illness of a pig, one of the stewards will be sufficient to decide whether or not the said pig shall be killed, but the whole must attend to decide on the loss.

9. That no member shall in any case have more than one pig in the club at a time, and that must not be a breeding sow, if known.

10. That in any case when the club shall come to a loss of two pounds, each member shall pay the sum of three-pence or extra if required to the collecting stewards and so on for every two pounds the stewards are to give notice of such loss to the members, and the fines to be the same in this case as in rule the third.

11. That any member imposing or attempting to impose on the club shall be immediately excluded.

12. That in case of the sudden death of a pig, the stewards shall give notice for the sale of the carcase, and the said pig to be sold to the best advantage within 24 hours for the benefit of the club.

13. That any new member after joining the club before becoming a free member, shall be entitled to one quarter of the value of the pig, if lost.

14. That no member shall feed and kill more than twenty score weight. in one year, on the risk of the club, unless recommended to do so by the stewards.

15. That all disputes shall be settled by ballot.

16. That the club hours are from 6 o'Clock until 8 p.m.

17. Any member insulting the stewards, or interrupting business in club hours, shall be fined for the first offence six-pence, second offence one shilling, and in default of payment, or third offence, to be excluded, and if disputed, to be settled by ballot, as in rule fifteenth.

18. That these rules shall be strictly attended to, and stand good until the next annual meeting.

E. BENNEY, Printer, ST. COLUMB.

The Rules of the St Merryn Pig Club, 1887. These rules in the form of a broadsheet would have been posted around the village to encourage the poor to join. In Victorian times the pig was a major outlay and primary source of food. The sudden death of a pig could be devastating for the family, so to offset such an occurrence pig clubs were formed and reimbursements made from their funds.

The foghorn at Trevose Lighthouse, c. 1913. The first foghorn was built in 1882 when the lighthouse was overhauled. Lord Rayleigh invented the new foghorn and it was inaugurated on the 6th February 1913. This immense structure measured 36 feet from top to bottom of the trumpet. In 1964 the foghorn was replaced by a visually less offensive structure.

The old Fish Cellars at Harlyn. The motto on the lintel above the door reads "Dulcis Lucri Odor" – profit smells sweet – an apt title, especially in the hot summer months! This building on the coastal path has been converted to a dwelling. The adjacent coastal footpath is badly marred by a growth of ugly signs. In May 1888 Mr Saunders of Sea View House saw a fish 4½ft in girth and 8ft in length. Believing it to be a whale, he ran to Harlyn Fisheries to get a harpoon. Here he met Capt. Bernhard Nelson and another person. They found the fish near the shore and harpooned it; after a struggle they pulled it ashore and found it to be a young sperm whale. It was then hiked about the countryside on show as far afield as St Columb. The Harlyn Fisheries were obviously equipped for every eventuality; in the foreground of the picture can be seen one of their seine boats.

Porthcothan Mill House, c. 1905. Below the house can be seen the roof of the mill itself, its water wheel being at the back of the mill building. On the hill to the left of the house is evidence of earlier buildings. Later dwellings were built up the hill from the mill house. In the background is Porthcothan Valley.

Porthcothan Mill, c. 1910. Notice the water wheel at the back of the mill building. Directly behind the mill is the side and roof of the mill house. Above the house are the newer houses. A public footpath wound down the hill past the back of the mill. On the skyline to the left is Porthcothan farmhouse and the site of the mill leat that fed the stream which powered this water mill.

Porthcothan, c. 1920. The large house on the hill is Trevethan farm, built in 1870 by Copplestone Cross, which was sold to the Andrew family before its completion. Below Trevethan on the shore is Beach Cottage, still owned by the Strongman family and partially converted to a shop. Far right is Glencoe, the home of the Darke family.

Cottages at Trevorrick Lane End, Porthcothan, c. 1885, since renovated and hardly recognisable in this photograph. The cherry tree was still *in situ* in 1927, but the shed on the right had gone prior to 1918.

104

A two horse cart loaded with seaweed on Porthcothan Bay, c. 1890. The seaweed was collected from the beach and transported to the fields and gardens, where it was used as an excellent and cheap form of fertiliser.

Autumn (c. 1890) on Trevethan Farm, Porthcothan. Mangolds are piled up into "caves" for the winter. The caves protected the mangolds from the frost, and were made by piling the mangolds into long apex-shaped mounds thatched with straw.

Seine fishing at Constantine Bay, c. 1906. The two girls in their warm winter coats are two of the three Harding sisters.

A good haul from a seine at Constantine, c. 1905. This photograph was taken under the cliffs just to the left of the entrance to the beach at Constantine. The Harding family, who owned a share in the seine, lived in the large house set back from the cliff path between Constantine and Treyarnon.

Squire and Mrs Old of Treyarnon Farm, c. 1900. This photograph is taken on a Feast Wednesday at Treyarnon Point. St Merryn Feast Sunday was traditionally the Sunday nearest to the 7th July. Feast week was a big occasion in the district and a time of much merriment as illustrated by the following extract from a newspaper of the 1880's. "Annual sports in connection with St Merryn Feast took place on Wednesday at Treyarnon Common, kindly lent by Mr J.B. Old for the purpose, and, the weather being fine, large numbers of persons from many miles around assembled. The principal event was the usual cricket match between Newquay and St Merryn teams, which resulted in favour of the visitors on the first innings, though in the second innings the home team had, when time was called, made a heavy score with six wickets to go down. After the match was concluded there were donkey races, running, and jumping. A public tea was provided for the parish, and was numerously patronised. The proceeds are to be devoted to a fund for the restoration of the parish church...."

St Merryn Cricket Team, 1931. Back row: Tremain Bennett, Clarence Strongman, Leadville Bennett, Alf Biddick (umpire), Cyril Ball, Harry Old. Middle row: Tremain Andrew, Harold Ball, Bert Harben, Ernest Old. Front row: Coulson Old, Pat Hellyar, Charlie Lobb. This team would have played against St Minver at Treyarnon Common on Feast Wednesday, a practice carried on until the outbreak of the Second World War.

St Merryn Cricket Team, c. 1880. At this time matches were played at Crigmorrick, near St Merryn Church, where this photograph was taken, as well as at Treyarnon.

Crigmorrick, c. 1900. This photograph shows the old cottage, which was later used as a barn but is now in a ruinous state. A stream, which is not visible in this photograph, ran across the road here, and a wooden bridge was built for pedestrians. In the background, on the higher ground, is St Merryn Church.

A group of itinerant travellers poses for a photograph on Treyarnon Common. A good selection of brooms are being offered, and a range of baskets and wickerware that reminds one of St Merryn's own basket maker, "Tiggy" Old, now based at Mellingey Mill; he doesn't have a goat, but he does have a llama!

St Merryn Football Team, c. 1948. Back row: Arthur Brown, Jack Mitchell, Arthur Brownhill, Trevor Scantlebury, Hubert Gregor, -?-, Neil Burke, Stanley Conium. Middle row: Jeff Mills, -?-, Alfred Osgood, Stanley Thomas, John Thomas. Front row: Clifford Newcombe, David Osgood and "Seaman" Penny.

Pentonwarra, Trevone, c. 1920. This house started life as a small cottage, and by the time this photograph was taken it had doubled in size to become a substantial residence overlooking Newtrain Bay, Trevone.

A view across Porthmissen Bay, c. 1930. Some years earlier, when Trevone was a cluster of houses half-way up the hill, the Prideaux Brune family went to the beach at Trevone accompanied by friends. The horses bolted, threw the coachman, and pulled the empty carriage homeward at speed, up the hill and around the winding roads to Trevone village. Here the carriage hit a hedge and broke off both rear wheels. The horses continued to drag the carriage for some distance, until Mr H.J. Champion, Mr R. Edwards and others, seeing what had happened, intercepted them. The coachman was only slightly injured, the horses had a few scratches, but the coach was very badly damaged.

The Cot Tea Rooms, Trevone, c. 1925. These rooms, once the old Methodist Chapel, are now a cottage.

Inside the Cot Tea Rooms, c. 1925. A pleasant ambience surrounded the patrons of seventy years ago, in this homely setting.

Newlands, Trevone, c. 1935. This plumbers shop was owned and run by Joseph Leonard Irons and Doris his wife from 1931 to 1945. Newlands is now a small hotel.

Eight
Military

The Home Guard of the St Eval and St Ervan Parishes during the Second World War. Top row: Charlie Powell, Ronald May, Andrew Johnson, Clifford Brewer, James Babb, Albert Ball, Preston Rabey, Reginald Chapman, Fred Cole, Jack Brenton, G. Brewer. Third row: R. Cocks, H. Chapman, Sidney Currah, Jack Rundle, Rowe Binney, Edward Gregor, N. Nicholas, Raymond Brewer, Eddie Hill, Frank Leverton, S. Brewer, Dennis Brewer, Frank Trebilcock. Second row: Walter Curtis, Harry Rundle, Richard Tremain, Bob Darke, Russell Brewer, H. Old, Jack Andrew, Harry Bennett, R. Bennett, George Morley, Leonard Curtis. Front row: Bertie Sandry, Wilfred May, G. Brewer, Harry Cowling, Warwick Cowling, William Key, Charles Curtis and Leonard Masters.

The crews of HMS *Conqueror* and HMS *Thunderer* are landing at the Custom House Slip, for the sailors to pay a goodwill visit to the town. The boat in the foreground is on the site of the present day sailing club. The Ice Factory and boatyard can be clearly seen in the background.

Members of the public waiting on the slip to board the steam launch, which towed the open boats on sight-seeing tours, circumnavigating the anchored warships at the Points.

HMS *Thunderer* lays off between the Points, while visitors are towed on their sightseeing visit.

The Market Place, July 1914. The flags are out, and all appear to be having a good time as the uniformed sailors are dined at the flower-adorned trestle tables.

One of the tables with sailors from HMS *Thunderer* and HMS *Conqueror*, sitting ready for their tea. The lady with the large hat on the left is Mrs Champion, with her grandson Bill in the white sailor suit worn especially for the occasion.

Padstow Home Guard 1914-1918 marching out of the Drill Hall opposite the Lawn. Colonel Prideaux Brune is leading the troop.

Padstow Artillery Volunteers with their gun at Battery. Annual inspections included this one made in September 1892: "The inspecting officers were Col. Hall Parlby RA, Capt. Mills RA, and Col. Gilbert. There was on parade Maj. Allport, Commanding Officer, Lt. Palk Griffin, Rev. Core (chaplain), Sgt. Inst. Hollowbone, and 60 men and non-commissioned officers. The company marched past, and was put through manual and firing exercises and company drill. Headed by the band, the corps marched to Coast Battery, where some good practice was made with 64-pounder R.M.L. on a moving target at a range of 2,000 yards. In the evening the annual supper took place at Mr Wills' "Commercial Hotel".

The Padstow Territorial Army gun crew at a competition at Falmouth. On the wheel of the gun carriage is painted "'A' Sub section No. 1 H.B. Cornwalls, Winning Team, Falmouth, 1911". The only member of the crew identified is my great-grandfather, Arthur Sidney May, and he is standing directly above the axle of the wheel carrying the inscription.

Broad Street, c. 1914. Hicks & Binney's shop can be seen in the background. A farrier checks the hooves of the horses which pulled the Territorials' field guns prior to their departure to war.

The horses that pulled the gun carriages used by the Artillery Volunteers line Broad Street in around 1914. Mr Hornabrook's blacksmiths shop can be seen in the background.

This is a photograph of the airship which was based at Crugmeer during 1918. A local resident recalls a bell ringing from this dirigible as it flew over Trehembourne. The dismantled mooring mast lay by the roadside near the Farmers' Arms, St Merryn for many years.

One of the RAF pilots sits in his plane at Crugmeer airfield; behind him is another biplane. The biplanes at the station comprised twelve DH6 coastal planes and, for a short time, a small number of Curtiss JN-4 Jenny training planes, but these were replaced by six DH9 biplanes.

Crugmeer was used as an airfield in the First World War. From the following aerial photographs an insight into the now defunct airfield can be gleaned. This photograph shows the hamlet of Crugmeer with the roof of Trethillick Farm house bottom left. The airfield was sited here as an anti-submarine base, the planes carrying two bombs on their routine two-hour patrols.

On the left is the road leading to Crugmeer and Trethillick; on the far side of the road can be seen the bell tents in which some of the 180 airfield personnel were billeted. The four bessoneaux hangars line the road to Porthmissen.

Biplanes outside the four bessoneaux hangers at Crugmeer Airfield. The airstrip was operational from March 1918 to March 1919. The landing strip was 1,500 feet long and faced into the prevailing winds.

On the left is the road from Crugmeer to Trethillick, and on the right the road to Lellizzick. The road to Porthmissen runs up to the top of the picture, with bell tents and wooden huts on the left. The hangars are just out of the top of the photograph. The airfield also had a tower for anchoring airships.

The ladies of the WVS St Merryn, c. 1942. These women in their smart green uniform and pinnies cooked meals and snacks for the men of HMS *Vulture*. Mrs Audrey Rabey recalls how they were taught to cook for large numbers of people using receptacles such as new dustbins, as well as the improvisations due to rationing, such as coffee from dandelion roots and salads made from plants growing wild in the local hedgerows. Another lady not in the photograph who was an active member was Mrs Gladys Gridley who, sadly, died in early 1994 aged 93. The ladies in the photograph are, back row: Mrs C. Brenton, Mrs Duffy, Mrs Gresswell, Mrs Ford, Mrs Prynn, Mrs Trevor Williams, Miss F. Barrett, Miss E. Chapman, Mrs Pollard. Front row: Miss Ruth Damerell, Mrs Needham-Cooper, Miss Eva Norris, Mrs Walker, Mrs Farquhar, Mrs Hicks, -?-, Miss Molly Sandry and Mrs E. Bellers.

One of the two Motor Torpedo Recovery Boats which were kept at Cove during the Second World War. These boats were used for clearing vessels from bombing sites; locally the sites were at Treligga and Kellan Head. The only uniformed persons on board were the two communications personnel.

Members of *Parkyn's Navy*. These men patrolled the area during the Second World War. The sailors are: Horace Murt, Bill Gamble, Tommy Morrissey, Frank Mabley, Bill "Foxy" Grant and "Muggy" Capp.

Parkyn's Navy. The vessels and crew are, from left to right: *Aileen*, with Jack England and Eric Martyn; *June*, with Bill Gamble and George Bennett; *Harmony*, with Tommy Morrissey (steering) and Donnie McBurnie Snr (engine room); *Kingfisher*, with Frank Mabley and Mr Piller from Brixham; *Stormcock*, with Horace Murt (skipper) and "Wiggy" Bennett; *Forget-me-Not*, with Bill Capp from Newlyn, and the *Ocean Pride*, with Jim Brownfield.

G Section, 202 Battery, 56 (Cornwall) HAA Regt. RA, at Rame Head heavy anti-aircraft gunsite, January 1940. This fine body of men in the Territorial Army were mobilized on 24th August 1939. They are, at the back: E. Gilmartin, Albert Kitto, Brenton Bate, Frank Caddy. Second row: Fred England, Douglas Martyn, Sidney Fuller, and, in the front, Bobby Dale.

202 Battery enjoy their Christmas dinner at Rame Head, December 1940. The Gunners are Jack Ingrey, an intake, Doug Martyn, an intake, -?-, Tom Mitchell, John Pitman, -?-, Willy Ellis, Brenton Bate and Owen Curtis.

"Wings for Victory" week, a smoking concert presented by the "Victory V Girls" in the Church Rooms. In the front: Daphne Nugent, Barbara Tonkin, Queenie Nugent, Joan Hoggitt, Marjorie Magor, Diane Palmer, Margaret Sorensen (the Chinese Mandarin), Kathleen Morrissey, and a woman from the Bodmin Fire Service. At the back: Eileen Nugent, Betty Chidgey, Mary Magor and Joan Bennett.

A "Wings for Victory" parade on Shop Crossroads, St Merryn, c. 1942. Standing at ease in front of the sailors from HMS *Vulture* is Cdr. Merlin Bruce RN. To the left of the matelots is PC Walke in his number one uniform and accompanying white gloves. The clergyman to the left centre is Rev. W. Bowden. Also to be seen in the crowd are Daphne Tippett, Joy Brewer, Audrey Driver and many more I am sure will be recognised.

PROGRAMME

11 A.M. UNITED SERVICE OF REMEMBRANCE
AND THANKSGIVING ON THE NORTH QUAY

2 P.M. WATER SPORTS IN THE QUAY

2.45 P.M. CONCERT ON THE QUAY

4.30 P.M. CHILDREN'S TEA IN THE MARKET
SQUARE

7 P.M. FANCY DRESS VICTORY PARADE

Parade will assemble at Prideaux Place
at 6.30 p.m.

**After the parade there will be
Dancing in the Market Square.**

11 P.M. HITLER'S EFFIGY WILL BE BURNT

in the Quay, and if possible there will
also be a Grand Firework Display
on the Quay.

After the Firework Display Dancing
will continue in the Market Square.

MID-NIGHT   -   -   -   **THE KING.**

Liddell and Son, Printers, Fore Street, Bodmin.

The Programme of Events for the Padstow Victory Day celebrations in 1946.

Souvenir Programme

of the

Padstow Victory Day

Celebrations

Saturday, 8th June, 1946

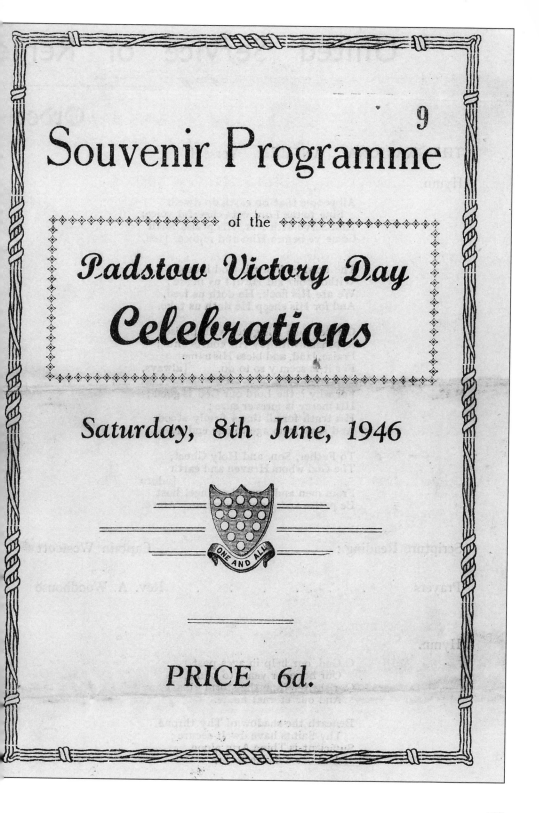

ONE AND ALL

PRICE 6d.

Acknowledgements

This book has been a pleasure to put together. A lot of this is due to the help and kindness of the people listed below, who have very kindly given or lent me photographs and supplied me with information necessary to the body of the book. Thank you all.

I must give one or two people a special mention: Jack Ingrey, a mine of information on St Merryn and district, a good friend and critical proof reader – cheers Jack; Mrs Molly Ball, for the photographs of Polmark Farm and the welcoming and kind reception given me by her and her late sister Mrs Gridley; Mrs Anita Rutherford and Ian for the use of her St Merryn photographs and their patience with my interrogations into the past – thanks. I would also like to thank Mrs Jane Bertuchi for photographs gratefully received of the Andrew family and the St Merryn, Porthcothan district. I must not forget my old stalwart, Mrs Margaret Brenton, who has helped and encouraged me for many years and somehow fits me in between her voluntary work. Thanks for your help Margaret; I am sure there are many people in the town that would like me to thank you for all you do for Padstow.

Tony Allen, Mrs Molly Ball, Mrs Irene Beavis, Mrs Chrissie Bennett, Mrs Hilda Bennett, Anthony and Jane Bertuchi, Derek and Jill Biddle, Mrs Ethel Blake, Mrs Margaret Brenton, Mrs Peggy Brunyee, Mrs (El)Freda Buckingham, Kevin and Mary Burke, Mr Alan Charles, Miss Betty Chidgey, Mr and Mrs Steven Colman, Mr Gordon Dawe, Mrs Millicent Denner, Joyce and Ken Dingle, Mr David Eddy, Mrs Sylvia Ellacott, Mrs Margaret Evans, Mr Clifton Fuller, Mr Harry Fuller, Mr Tom Gard, Bob and Janet Gerkin, Katherine Grice, Mrs Marjorie Grubb, Mrs Jean Haige, Mr Hampton, Mrs Joyce Hibbert, Mr Geoff Hicks, Mr and Mrs Robert Hicks, Capt. George Hogg, Mr Keith Holloway, Miss Cynthia Hoskin, Mr Jack Ingrey, Mrs Madeline Keat, Mr and Mrs Melville Kestell, Rev. Barry Kinsmen, Mrs Helen Langford, Mr Tony Magor, Mr Douglas Martyn, Mr Jack Martyn, Pat, Lionel, Sheila and Eric McCarthy, Mr Tommy Morrissey, Freddie Murt, Mr Steven Murt, Mr David Old, Terry "Tiggy" Old, Mr Alfie Orchard, Padstow Echo, Mrs Vera Pawley, Fred and Molly Pinch, Mr George Phillips, Mrs Audrey Rabey, Mr Donald Rawe, Mrs Mary Redding, Mrs Eileen Rossiter, Ian and Anita Rutherford, Mr A.M. Sheppard, Mrs Marjorie Trenouth, Mrs Walker, Mrs Phillippa Wearden, Mr Sedwin Wills, Mr John Wilton.